www.finishinglinepress.com

In The Throes of Beauty

poems by

Kevin LeMaster

Finishing Line Press
Georgetown, Kentucky

In The Throes of Beauty

ACKNOWLEDGMENTS

I would like to thank the following publications in which some of these
poems, either in their current form or another form, first appeared.
*Slipstream, Main Street Rag, Hive Avenue Literary Journal, Barely South
Review, Mantis, Flying Island Review, Coffin Bell Journal* and *BigCityLit*.

I'd also like to thank Kari Gunter Seymour for including my poem, "Toll
Takers 1972" in the anthology *I Thought I Heard a Cardinal Sing*,
Taylor Mali, Vicky Mullen Adkins, Nancy Coates Posey, Michael Burns,
Katlyn Burns and Hallee Boals for reviewing my manuscript with a fine
tooth comb, Katlyn Burns for creating the beautiful cover and my wife Nelda
for loving me throughout the process.

I'd also like to thank all my poetry friends, Daniel Edward Moore,
Francesca Bell, Taylor Mali, Jerod Singer, Nicole Homer and Bianca Phipps
for their continued support and friendship.

Publisher: Leah Huete de Maines
Editor: Christen Kincaid
Cover Art: Katlyn Burns
Author Photo: Taylor Mali
Cover Design: Elizabeth Maines McCleavy

Order online: www.finishinglinepress.com
also available on amazon.com

Author inquiries and mail orders:
Finishing Line Press
PO Box 1626
Georgetown, Kentucky 40324
USA

Contents

Skipping stones from the edge of a River in Kentucky

I favor the smooth round ones,
prefer the musty smell of river rocks

to the glimmer of quartz or fool's gold.

some stay buried right where my toes
can find them,

others fit just right between thumb and
forefinger and when I

hold my arm like this, I can let one
sail like a small bird

hesitantly spreading its wings for the
first time, then another and another

until it skips like a young girl along
a sidewalk in any suburb.

the river's expanse is not as vast as the ocean's
ebb, but then, being from Kentucky, how would

I know such things? How would I understand
just how far the ocean wave can take you,

except being one who floated way past
the barrier of buoy and rope, like a stone

that had exhausted all its skips, at risk of sinking,
moored only by the weight of its own fear.

Toll Takers 1972

From the road, you can no longer see
the hut where the old men stayed when
there was no one waiting to press the small tan
and red ticket into a willing withered palm,
just to gain entrance to the tall steel girded bridge
that spanned the Ohio.

Dressed in their cotton white tee and suspenders,
wreathed in thick gray smoke from their black
bowled pipes, chatting about Rainbow Trout
biting up river, and a time when bridges
would be free access and patrons could
come and go as they pleased.

I can see them laughing at the absurdity, some spitting
tobacco juice into a spittoon on the floor next to them,
others clutching their pipes for dear life,
like holding the past in their bare hands.

Years have passed and there is nothing left of the building,
like a bruise that fades and is gone. The road has turned
from two lanes to four and the old steel girders
have yielded to a newer suspension bridge.

If you listen close you can still hear the wind
ask, Tickets please? If you inhale deeply,
you can still smell their tobacco,
circling the air like a ghost.

Bees carry their food to an undisclosed location

they congregate on our porch
like neighbors who refuse to leave
crawl into a soda awaiting a ready
mouth

this one is carrying a fly between his muscled
legs in route to prepare what looked like dinner
a reservation for one and out of respect
for hunger, I let him live today

as if I was his reprieve when
in fact I just decided it was necessary
not to end him, nature being
what it is and since lunch

hadn't made it to its final destination
who am I to hamper a creature's
digestion, who am I to save
something who had already given

in to the idea of being eaten
remaining motionless, neither
resisting or succumbing
just spending his last few

moments being, without making a show
about it

What dying becomes

the blossoms are falling
from dying vines
as morning

hangs in suspended animation;
dewdrops laced across tired
withering leaves.

a mist of rain makes a sound
like cicada's waining call,
their hulls falling

feather-like to the ground.
A collection of dead
trophies line

the garden path, a burial pyre
of empty bodies crunch
under the tenderest step

and I am caught waiting
for everything to die,
the leaves being last

to the funeral, covering
all that is left in a dark
moldy brown, waiting

for the resurrection of Spring
when new life grows from desolation

What we no longer say

In early Appalachia, when a poultice
was applied, it had to stay

there for days. they said it would draw
the growth to the surface,

like a fish to a baited hook; life struggling
on a taut line. the fight

was almost more than grandfather
could bear,

when it was removed a week later
his upper lip came off with the cancer.

afterward, he grew a mustache
to hide what was missing

and lived the remainder of his life
well into his nineties,

his upper lip preserved in a jar
on a shelf above his bed,

just in case he had
something more to say.

Carry

he wears the world
like a torn coat

uncomfortable with
how the sleeves

ride to the elbow how tight
the shoulders feel

when he moves too much.
He dreams of when a 42 long,

fit comfortably and tattered
things were something told

that didn't seem like lies;
 this world, a swallow of dry

leaves. He dreams of the day
when black men can live

without the fear of a bullet
tattooing the chest

of everyone they love, their necks
bent toward hell.

a day when no one will walk
into a supermarket and open fire

in the produce section behind
the deli. he is like a boy with a tiny

wounded bird cradling the world
in his arms,

stroking its tired feathers and nursing
it back to health

so it can raise more white sons to kill again.
this coat grows smaller with each wear,

full of holes and bleeding the same red.

Pinch and Dash

mom never measured ingredients, everything
was all pinch and dash, all taste and taste
again and when cookies came out
of the oven, you knew they were right
by the smell wafting under your nose
like a spell.

those same hands used to hold my face,
smacked us away from the hot dough,
baked to perfection like a magic trick
performed well, one anyone can learn.

a good magician never reveals
her secrets but I never learned
the importance of listening in time.

A dog named dinner

He laid still in the mouth
of the Legion field,

and I thought him dead, the dog,
more animated,

nuzzled his way out from under
the ratty black tarp

used as a blanket. they made camp
in an abandoned patch of uncut grass

a sheet of spring rain halted
their travels south,

Georgia bound on foot, hitchhiking
through every stranger's

town from here to there. Dinner's
coat was immaculate,

a smooth black and white
resembling spun silk.

his master, educated, wrapped
three hardback books

up with the rest of his belongings,
carrying everything they owned

in the rough tarp they slept under,
rolled and bundled with jute.

he talked about where he came
from, how far he was going,

about the journey, and Dinner, his adoring
eyes glistening in the morning sun,

looking up, hungry

Well Fed

those bloated bellies hanging
out after picking chicken

to the bone, stripping ribs
like a pro, one handed

teeth lain bare against the marrow
of another cleaned rack

portion control don't work here
we may be hicks but larger hearts

don't necessarily mean a lack
of other things

home cooking means
you can pull up a chair

even if your nails have never dug the earth
even if you don't eat with your hands
even if you're not family

we can teach you

Snapping Beans After Church

We used to break beans
by the bucket, snap both ends
like breaking a chicken's neck
when it would get fat from the grain.

mom would sing hymns off key
and we would hum their tired
refrains clear into the evening.

after dusk you could smell the aroma
of half runners, pressure cooking
on the stove, the gentle shu shu shu
of the jiggler releasing steam
and the aroma of fried chicken
sizzled in hot cast iron.

grease popped like the gun cousin
Tom used, the .25 gauge with the pearl
handle, deep in those woods behind
the house, and we kept calling for him
to come and eat,

but only the crickets replied.

On the Forest Floor

a young deer crawls to a shallow ditch,
grazed by the wheel of a whining
Harley Davidson.

not a fatal blow, his side already pierced
by the hunter's bullet, but enough
to cause a small stream of bright red

to trickle down the dirt path and pool around
a young pine sapling. nature takes care
of its children and as the sound pulls

away from the forest's ear, her eyes close,
the leaves pull up around her
and she drifts off to sleep.

Ladybug

The leafy green
surrounds the tiny
bicycle helmet
spotted
orphaned by some
lost thing
species unknown
wandering around
unsafe
in the midst
of all this beauty

Learning to Fly in One Easy Step

As the sun rises
over the fresh
red pavement

I wonder how long
you stood

on that high ledge
before you decided

to take your first
flying lesson

and if I could have reached
you in time

The Art of Plums

we used to paint the house
with their rotten bodies

watch as they splatter against cinder
block and window. the harder

we threw them, the louder the sound
like the flutter of broken wings

as they fly toward something terrible
their dark yellow flesh

would dry in the noonday
August sun

sticking in all the porous cracks
and crevices of the mortar

making something unsightly,
more like a forgotten Pollock

than a mischievous child's prank
and my mother would cry

between words until we spent the rest
of the day, scrub brush in hand,

cleaning every crack until the house
glistened when the sunlight hit it just right

Valentine

a paper lace cutout,
made with safety
scissors and Elmer's

glue graces our fridge
with I Love You stenciled
in its heart-shaped

cleft. my grandson knows
forever has no end
and that's how long

he wants to see his handiwork
displayed. every time
the light illuminates

the milk when the door
is open he wants to see
his heart

hanging in the half light
of early dawn, vulnerable
and visible

for all the world to see.

Without These Things

In my hemisphere
starlight is mostly
obscured by clouds,

no sitting or lying on a bed
of luxurious Kentucky blue
to see Orion's Belt or squinting

to see the line of stars
that make up the big
dipper. oak leaves

swirl like antique light, crackling
fissures revealing a teal blue sky;
a vase with varicose

veins, stretching the limits of
its porcelain torso. we try
and ground ourselves

by the north star and wonder
where the rest have hidden,
without these things,

we would not feel the pull
of their inherent beauty,
appreciated like the shape

of clouds; pig ear and cotton
candy, elephant and dove.
without these things

you wouldn't have radiated so bright,
burning out like a match, struck
against the world.

To Dust

the weeds have overtaken
its block walls, dragging
the bones down

through tendrils of grass; thousands
of tiny fingers reaching higher
until all that is left is its dark

green wake. its insides smell
of black mold and musty
cigarettes, dingy walls
evidenced by the smokers

who lived there; three packs a day
cradled in the hand, sporting
the long yellow nail.

its walls run with rainstorms,
trickling down the dated paneling
and onto the concrete floor

and I am a belly full of stones, river worn
and waterlogged, full of hurt and longing.
a house well lived with all its secrets

is soon to be buried with its memories,
underneath the garden with the dogs
and the hamster, mummified and wrapped

in a white cheese cloth that emerged
from the rich earth during planting
season, the bleached bones white

as stars on a warm summer night.

Skin the Cat

I never was much good
at getting my legs tucked
enough to flip

upside down and stick
the landing, so I hung
there among the swirl

of leaves and crabgrass,

until all I could see
was the blurred
image of the catawba

scattering its cigar

shaped buds all over
the yard. Dad would
always make me rake

them into a pile and dump
them over the back fence
but I had to practice

so I wouldn't be the only kid
late back from recess
unable to be rescued

from my own fear
of being different
unable to stand

on my own two feet

The Low Hum of Strange Music

the gas pumps behind my house
simultaneously bellow

like the closing prayer during Sunday's
service, young me squirming for an end

that seems to go on forever. yet I go
inside anyway, mesmerized, top off

my tank and buy a coffee. the local
newspaper tells of another overdose

just in back of the Speedway across
the river and I am unable to react

anymore. welcome to new small town
America, just a place to live and die,

with nothing in between.still, the pumps hum,
fill us with false hopes of prosperity,

of commerce, of feelings of something
you can't buy here.

Groundhog

another day where growing
shadows fall

promising six more weeks
of packed white

earth. small strips of dirt
peek through like fools

gold, rich dark veins
springing forth,

just as everything awakens
anew and fragrant.

flowers dance with eyes
closed, in a soft breeze.

johnny cakes make
in hot cast iron,

golden and crispy.
a child holds one

like other's hold candy,
for this is Appalachia

and we are born with corn
pone in our mouths

and the taste of soup beans
smacking on our lips.

right now the snow falls,
giving way for the groundhog

to make his important decision,
and like superstition dictates

we respect it and dress accordingly,
like everyday is groundhog day.

Catching the Sunday special

they kept their milk
under the porch

and fresh coffee
boiling on the wood stove

as a welcome and a mercy
a hobo approached

the small sharecropper shack
weary from the cold boxcar

asking for sugar, for milk
for a spoon

and as he leaned back

in that old rickety chair
legs worn to nubs

my angered grandfather
kicked

it out from under him
for expecting too much

of their hospitality
they kept their milk

under the porch because
that was the coolest spot

against the heat of the sun
and for the next hobo

who would ride the rail
to the end of the line

be careful what you ask
for in a Kentucky holler

with no escape save
the road

or the grave

When the weather called for Ice and all we got was rain

at night when rain
comes down like
flocks of crows,

blanketed in black,
an onyx reflection
that goes on for miles,

ice forms in the upper atmosphere
making the land a crystal ocean of
disbelief and we listen to the sound

of the collected widening,
until the water is all we see.

cars lose ground and float
away, while babies cry.
mothers discuss loss

over bridge or crochet,
stitching clothes to forget,
darning socks because

that's all they know to do.
loss is the greatest creation,
something that happens

miraculously without explanation
or warning, making us miss
those closest to us.

loss means never again to find
what's missing, which is to say
the pieces no longer fit.

remember to say their names
quietly, reverently.

What happens in a level two snow emergency

Snow falls through
the quiet trees

trickles down, meeting
the ground in secret

like a forbidden lover
who lies down beside

them and whispers
that they will

be together forever
but leaves in Spring

without a word

10,000 hours (or the time it takes)

Someone once said that's how long
It takes to   be good at

      Anything   like poetry
I started late   destined in my forties

to be still trying at seventy   experienced already
in dying   life   and children

I have the art of walking   down   with a precision of
Steps   and movement that mimic

A waltz without music   and talking
Was a birth of love

like a train pulled from
a tunnel   all that sound

pulsing with life

a unique practice   of love
      unrequited   stings like

Ripping flies   from their wings
making me an artist   of sorts

Now   being great at poetry
      Will have to wait till I almost
forget   what it is like

To be so clever   forget alliteration
Or rhyme   or song

10,000 hours   27 years   maybe ill be
as great   as a flower in   an empty field

Sunday Church

Sunday mornings were always
all biscuits, gravy
and rhubarb.

I would dip a bit of both
out of the large white bowls
onto the Corning Ware plates

and would spoon a little of each
on exactly two halved biscuits
breakfast and desert in one.

Dad would dress all in black like holding on
to sin and God at the same time,
the bible clutched tightly

in his right hand. The cover was worn
and the gold embossed pages
were a dingy yellow.

Mom dressed in bold, flower-print
dresses, never below the knee
like the church commanded,

but tastefully short and modest.
she followed the staunch shadow
of a man devoutly and without question.

His indiscretions opened like the very pages
he desperately sought for answers
to life's problems,

sitting the pew waiting for the minister
to make a mistake,
constantly stuck

in the book like a fly that won't leave
you alone until you slam
the pages shut

breaking spirit and body
with one quick action,
shortening life by hours.

proving people wrong, provided
countless arguments in
the back of an almost

empty church, until someone
went home mad and I, understanding
little about the man I thought he was,

went home hungry and tired,
Usually expecting a whipping
over something I had done,

and getting it.

Ringer

Any self-respecting Kentuckian
would spit through the arc
of a horseshoe

before throwing it for luck, so when I asked
my wife if her father did the same
thing, I already knew the answer was yes.

We talked about my uncle
who had to have a Styrofoam cup
dangling at the end of the stake

so he could see to ring it.
She said that her father was
that good too and now needed

the same courtesy, and when he gave
all his pocketknives to me, I knew
I had to play horseshoes

with him if just to get him to try something again,
because giving up is a lot like those broken
knives,

no matter how tempered the blade
you're only as strong as the metal
you're forged with,

and when you hear it ring true
you know its sound.

Kevin lives in Northeastern Kentucky with his wife of thirty-six years. Writing has alway been a passion of his, but not completely realized until his early forties when he joined a group of older poets known as The Phoenix Writers, from there he took the advice of seasoned poets and honed his craft with a deeper understanding of poetry and the elements that make up a good poem.

Kevin learned from many individuals in his poetry journey, primarily through Daniel Edward Moore and Taylor Mali was he able to grow and become the poet he is today. He believes that a poet never stops learning or believing in the poetry he creates. If we lose our humility, we've lost our humanity.

Kevin's poems have been found at *SheilaNaGig* online, *Gyroscope Review, Hive Avenue Literary Journal, Main Street Rag, Barely South Review, Mantis, Amistad* and others. Kevin has work forthcoming in *Appalachian Places Magazine* and *BigCityLit Journal*. His second chapbook *In The Throes Of Beauty* (Finishing Line Press) is forthcoming.

Kevin is the author of the chapbook *Mercy* (Arroyo Seco Press, 2023) and has been nominated for a Pushcart twice and once for a Best of Net.

www.ingramcontent.com/pod-product-compliance
Lightning Source LLC
Chambersburg PA
CBHW022052080426
42734CB00009B/1310